TO DONNA:

HOPE YOU GET MUCH ENJOYMENT FROM THIS STORY. I'M GLAD TO HAVE MET YOU.

The Raging, Flaming Goat of Samos

Michael J. Andrade

The Raging, Flaming Goat of Samos

© 2012 Michael J. Andrade

ISBN: 978-1-61170-087-9

All rights reserved. No part of this publication may be reproduced, stored in a retrieval system or transmitted in any form or by any means, electronic, mechanical, photocopies, recording or otherwise, without the prior written consent of the author.

Printed in the USA and UK on acid-free paper.

Robertson Publishing™
59 North Santa Cruz Avenue
Los Gatos, California 95030 USA
www.RobertsonPublishing.com

The Raging, Flaming Goat of Samos

Many years ago, when the moon was still made of cheese and life was full of magic, there lived a goat and a cat.

Michael J. Andrade

Sure, there lived a lot of other things too.
But try to focus on these two, okay?

The Raging, Flaming Goat of Samos

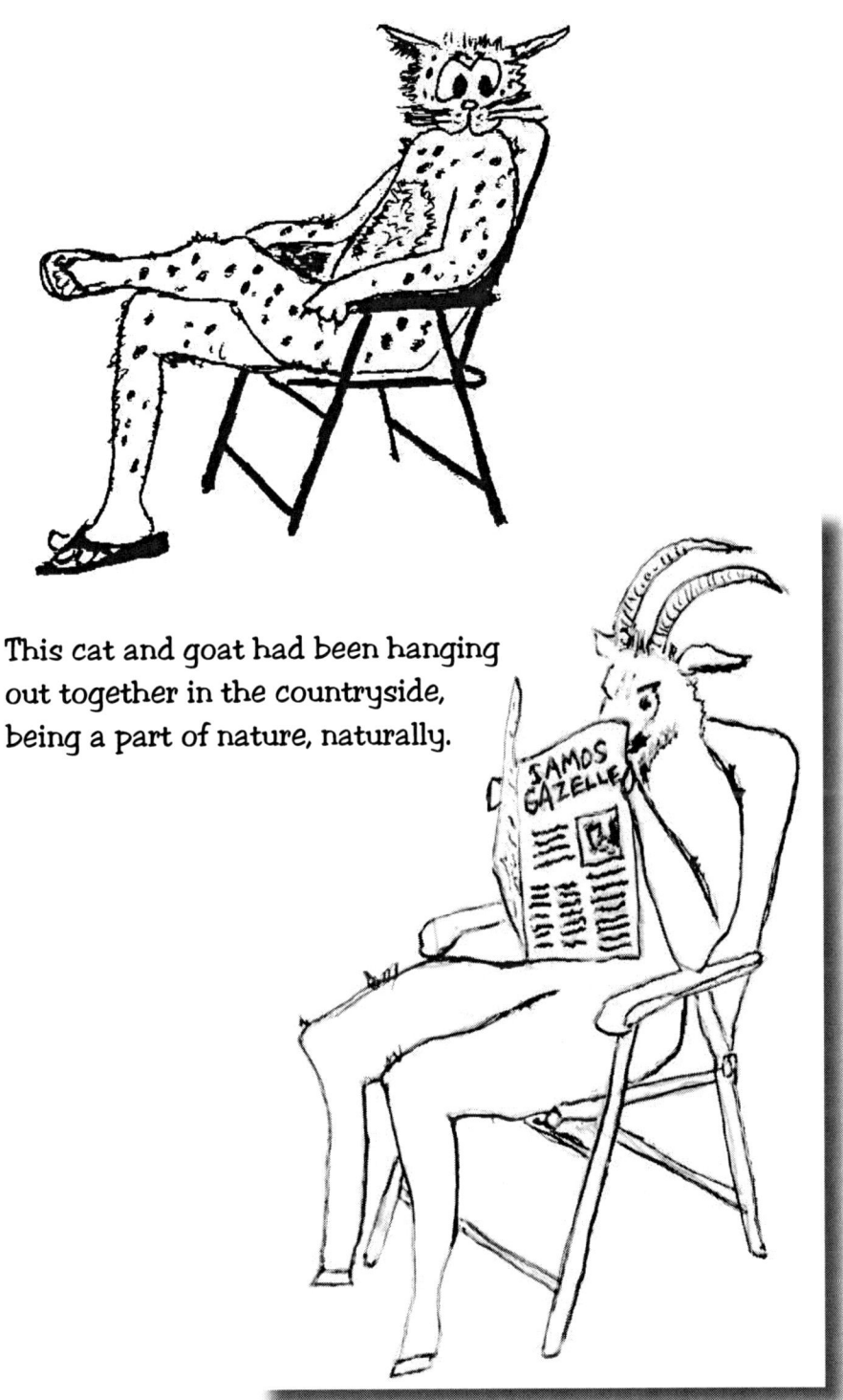

This cat and goat had been hanging out together in the countryside, being a part of nature, naturally.

Michael J. Andrade

On this particular day, the cat had reached a turning point. He asked the goat, "Do you think I'm crazy?"

"Why do you say that?" said the goat.

"I can't seem to put my claw on it," said the cat.

"You're just a mild mannered cat," said the goat.

But the cat heard differently. "Yes!" he said. "I'm wild! I'm a wild animal! That's it exactly!"

And with that, the cat reared up, pounced on the goat, and swallowed him in one gulp.

"I said mild!" said the goat, muffled as if wrapped in blankets. "Let me out of here!"

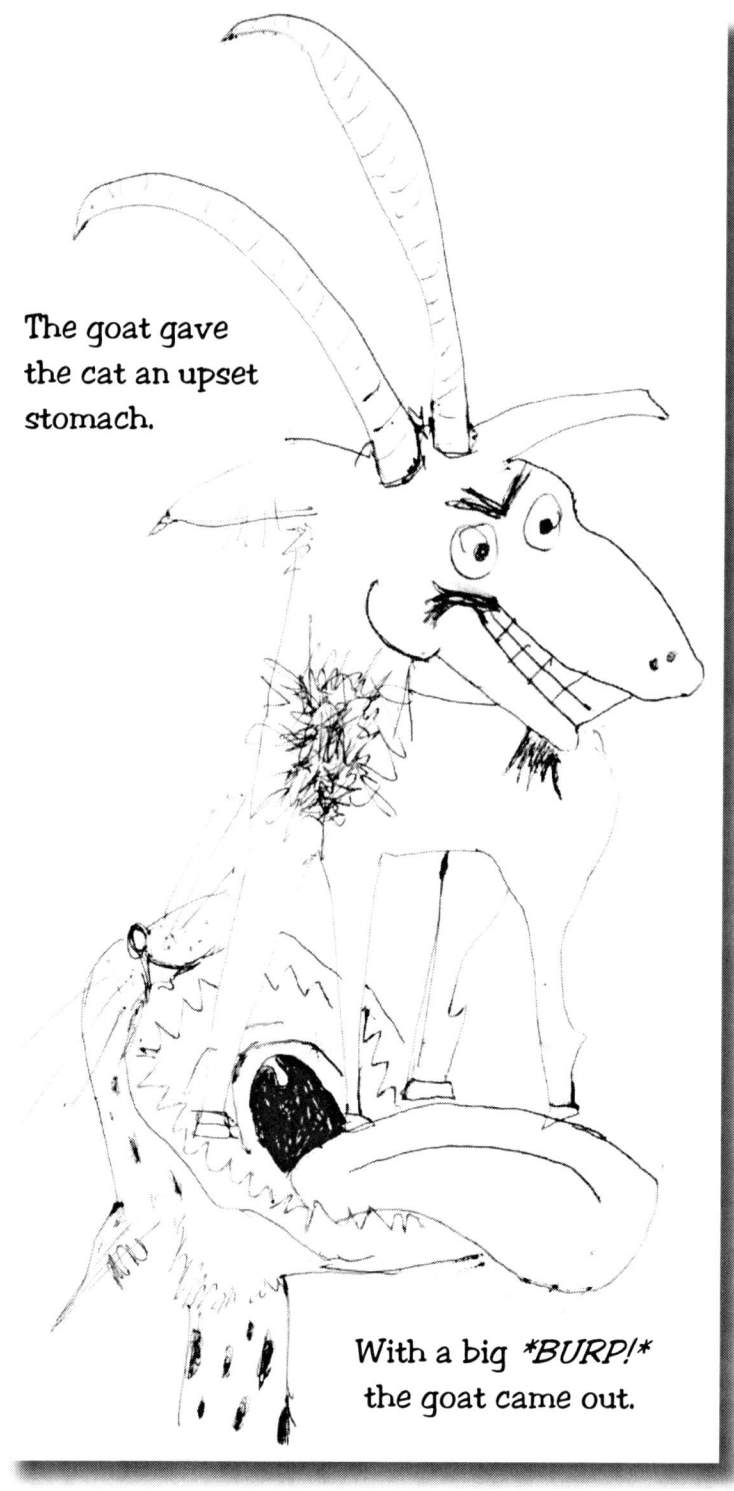

The goat gave the cat an upset stomach.

With a big *BURP!* the goat came out.

The Raging, Flaming Goat of Samos

"Why'd you do that?" yelled the goat,
his temper and temperature rising.

"I'm sorry. I had to. I better go," said the cat. He packed his spots and left.

The goat's horn started to smoke.
"Some friend you are!" he yelled.
His anger made him hot.

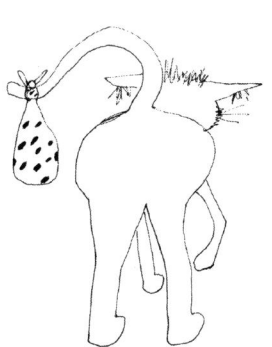

Being gobbled up and spit out like so much bad licorice had left a foul taste in his mouth. *A good taco will help me feel better,* he thought.

The Raging, Flaming Goat of Samos

The goat walked over to the taco cart. The smoke from the goat's horn got in the taco man's eye. "Would you like something cold to drink?"

"No," said the goat. "Gimme a couple veggie tacos."

"Hot or mild salsa?"

"MILD!" yelled the goat.

"Mild it is," said the taco man. With the smoke in his eye, the taco man grabbed the wrong salsa.

"Sir, this is a non-smoking restaurant," he said.

"I'll take it to go then," snarled the goat, his head burning.

The goat walked for a bit, then chomped both tacos with nary a chew. The hot salsa began to ignite in his mouth and throat. He got hotter, and more agitated.

He began to gallop around,
kicking, bucking, and screaming.

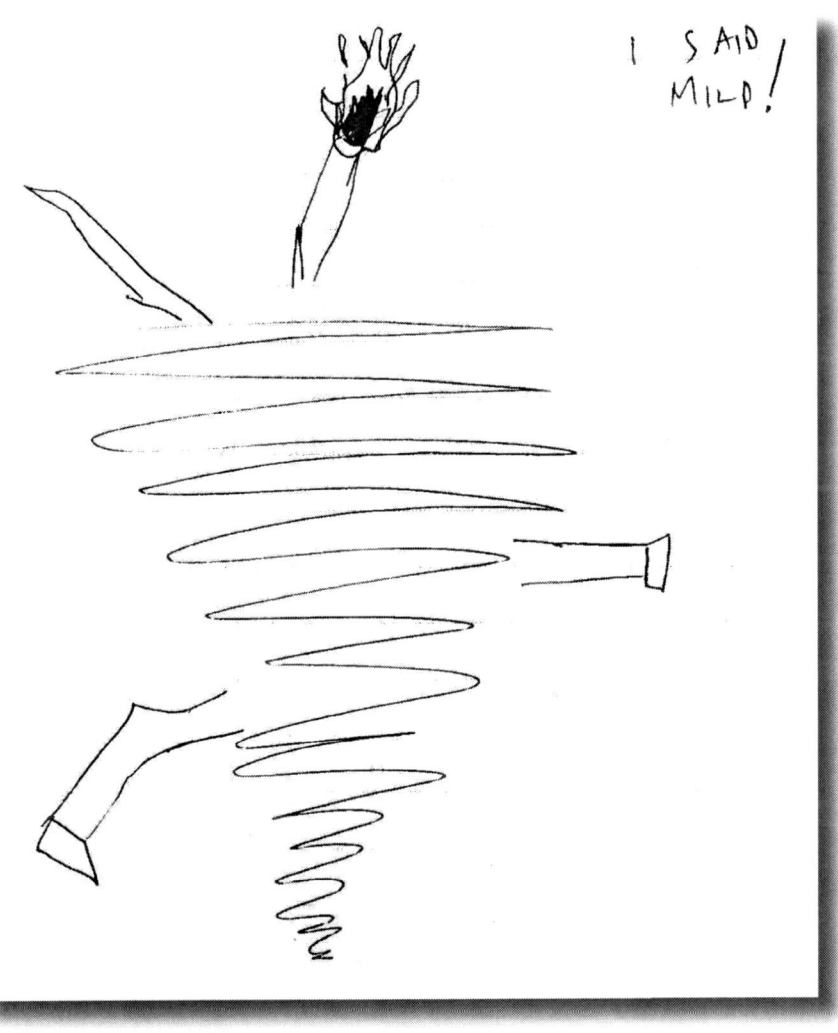

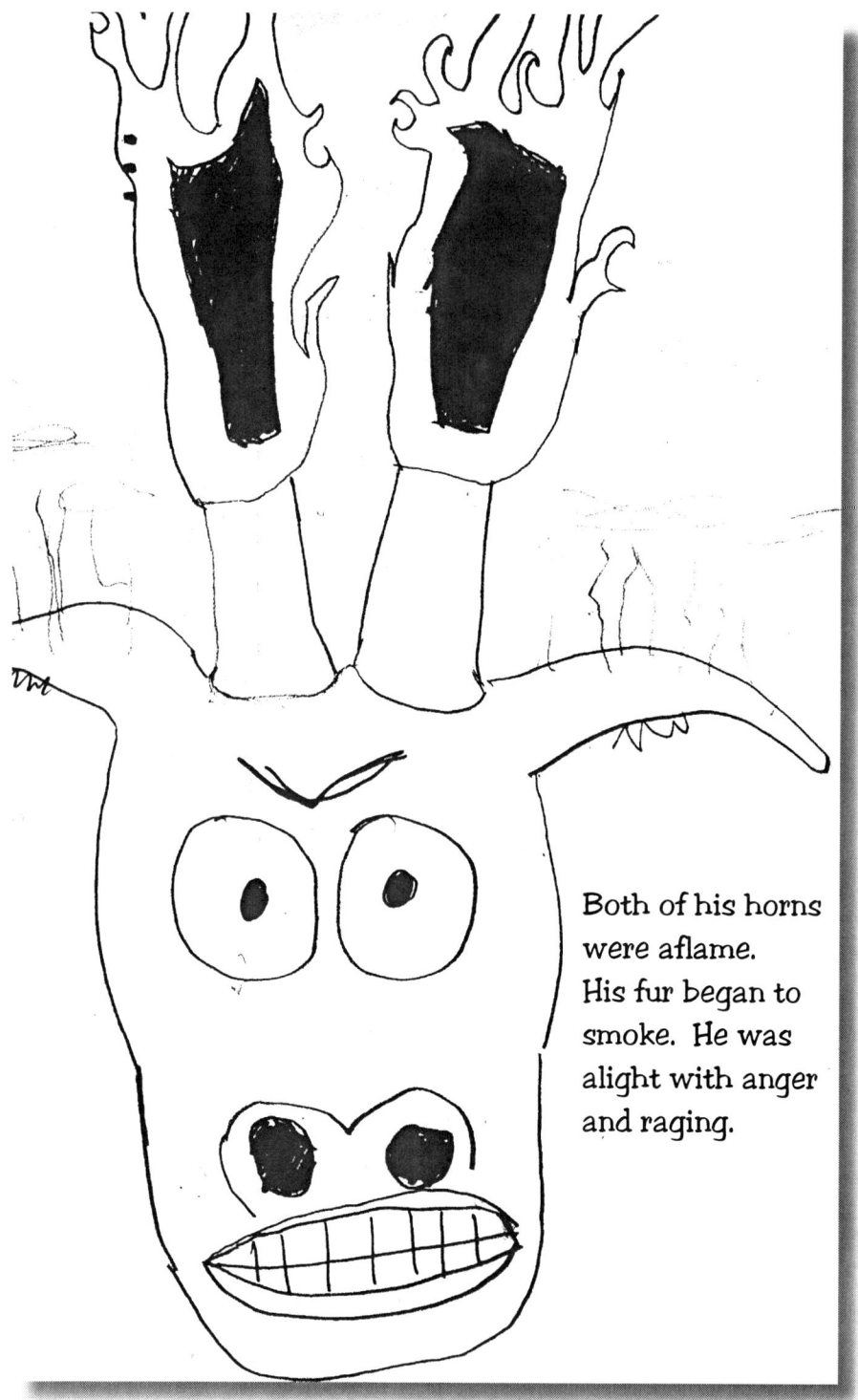

Both of his horns were aflame. His fur began to smoke. He was alight with anger and raging.

He climbed to the top of a hill and tried to catch his breath. He was so mad! His temper burned like his horns.

He was truly a hot head. In frustration, he stomped, and the ground gave way.

He fell into a cave. When the dust settled, he couldn't believe his eyes.

"What are YOU doing here?" yelled the goat.

"I'm stuck," said the wild cat of Samos. "The townspeople chased me in here, then barricaded the entrance."

"What? Why?" said an exasperated goat.

"I've got a reputation for swallowing livestock, I guess," offered the cat.

"You gotta get a hold of your emotions, man!" yelped the goat.

"You should talk, Smokey."

The two stopped and looked up.

The Raging, Flaming Goat of Samos

"Ahoy!" said Gerasimos. "I will subdue this wild cat!"

"I must liberate the townspeople
from your reign of terror."

"If you must," said the cat.

Gerasimos sprung at the cat and missed, ran into the goat, and singed his eyebrows.

The goat lost his temper. "I've gotta get out of here!" he yelped.

He grabbed the rope to climb out of the cave. He strained and pulled and huffed and puffed. His horns burned bright; his mane smoldered. He struggled up the rope. It took all of his might and strength to keep going.

As he climbed, he felt like he was getting heavier.
He was so mad! And the anger weighed on him.

He kept pulling but he just couldn't do it.
He thought he might lose his grip and fall.

Instead of letting go of the rope, he let go of the anger.
As he pulled himself up over the rim, he began to cry.

His tears doused the flames that were raging in and on him. In no time he was a charred smoking black lump of coal, hissing with evaporating steam.

The cat and Gerasimos watched in awe as the goat separated himself from the glowing embers of the crusty, fiery burden of his anger.

The goat helped the man and the cat climb out of the cave. The three of them stood for a moment and stared at the charred exoskeleton of the goat, a smoldering symbol of his anger.

"So that's the Raging, Flaming Goat of Samos, eh?" said Gerasimos. "Yeah," said the cat.

"Tacos are on me," said the goat, and they all walked together back towards the taco cart.

Legend has it that the crusty exoskeleton of the Raging, Flaming Goat of Samos can still be seen from certain parts of the island, as it smolders, glowing in amber light to this day.

CPSIA information can be obtained at www.ICGtesting.com
Printed in the USA
BVOW022335131112

305470BV00006B/23/P

9 781611 700879